READING POWER

Writing in the Ancient World

WRITING IN ANCIENT MESOPOTAMIA

JIL FINE

The Rosen Publishing Group's
PowerKids Press™
New York

Published in 2003 by The Rosen Publishing Group, Inc.
29 East 21st Street, New York, NY 10010

First Edition

Book Design: Michael DeLisio

Photo Credits: Cover, p. 20 © Réunion des Musées Nationaux/Art Resource, NY; p. 4 © SEF/Art Resource, NY; pp. 5, 12, 13 Michael DeLisio; p. 6 © Nick Wheeler/Corbis; pp. 7 (top), 8, 12 © Eric Lessing/Art Resource, NY; pp. 7 (middle, bottom left, bottom right), 15 © Scala/Art Resource, NY; pp. 9, 16, 17 © Gianni Dagli Orti/Corbis; pp. 10–11, 14 © Bettmann/Corbis; pp. 18–19, 21 © The Granger Collection

Library of Congress Cataloging-in-Publication Data

Fine, Jil.
Writing in ancient Mesopotamia / Jil Fine.
   p. cm. — (Writing in the ancient world)
ISBN 0-8239-6509-0 (lib. bdg.)
1. Cuneiform writing—History—Juvenile literature. 2. Sumerian language—Writing—Juvenile literature. 3. Akkadian language—Writing—Juvenile literature. 4.
Writing—Iraq—History—Juvenile literature. [1. Iraq—Civilization—To 634. 2. Writing—History.] I. Title. II. Series.
PJ3193 .F56 2003
492'.111—dc21

                                           2002002924

Contents

MESOPOTAMIA

The world's earliest civilization began in the area called Mesopotamia. People started living there around 10,000 B.C. The land in Mesopotamia was very good for farming.

These stones were part of a building in an ancient civilization in Mesopotamia near the Euphrates River.

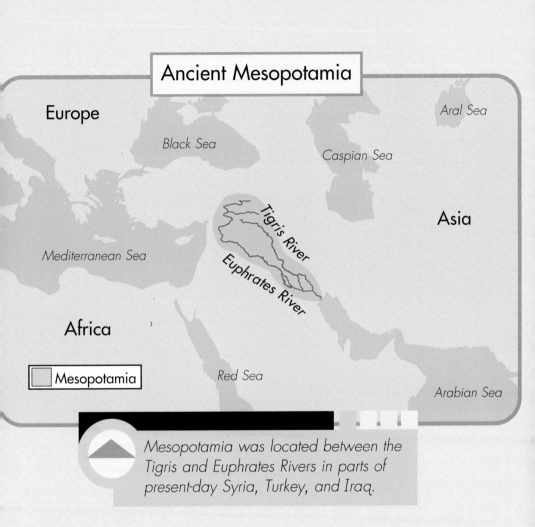

Ancient Mesopotamia

Europe

Aral Sea

Black Sea

Caspian Sea

Asia

Tigris River

Euphrates River

Mediterranean Sea

Africa

☐ Mesopotamia

Red Sea

Arabian Sea

Mesopotamia was located between the Tigris and Euphrates Rivers in parts of present-day Syria, Turkey, and Iraq.

CHECK IT OUT

▶ Mesopotamia (meh-suh-puh-TAY-mee-uh) means "land between the rivers" in the Greek language.

The first cities in the world were built in Mesopotamia around 3500 B.C. by the Sumerians *(soo-MEHR-ee-uhnz)*. Around the same time, the Sumerians also invented the first system of writing.

Many Sumerian cities were so well-built that they are still standing today.

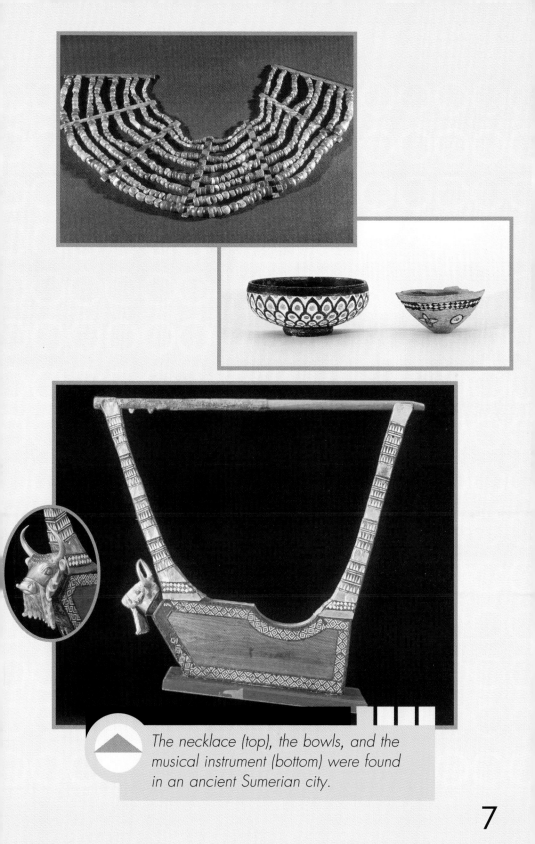

The necklace (top), the bowls, and the musical instrument (bottom) were found in an ancient Sumerian city.

THE FIRST SYSTEM OF WRITING

The Sumerians first used writing to keep records of goods that were owed or traded. They used a pointed stick to draw pictures of the goods on tokens, or small pieces of clay.

There were more than 1,200 pictures used in early Sumerian writing.

If a man traded three sheep, a bookkeeper would draw a picture of a sheep on each of three different tokens. The tokens would be kept in a clay jar or a bag made of cloth or leather. Sometimes, the pictures on the tokens were also drawn on the outside of the jar. Then, people did not have to open the jar to see what was inside.

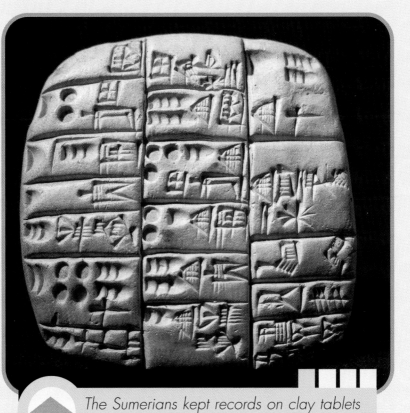

The Sumerians kept records on clay tablets about the number of goats and sheep they owned or traded.

The Sumerians soon made a way to write numbers. Bookkeepers stopped using tokens to record trading. Instead, bookkeepers made a picture of the item to be traded on a wet clay tablet. They also made a picture to show the number of items in the trade.

Bookkeepers had to be careful when making pictures and numbers in clay tablets. Sloppy signs could be misread.

CUNEIFORM

In time, the Sumerians used a wedge-shaped stick called a stylus to make characters in the clay tablets. The stylus had a tip that was shaped like a triangle.

This Sumerian tablet is a record of the sale of a field and a house.

CHECK IT OUT

Cuneiform *means "wedge shape" in the Latin language.*

12

The characters were made up of wedges that were wide at one end and pointed at the other end. Each character represented an entire word. The writing was called cuneiform.

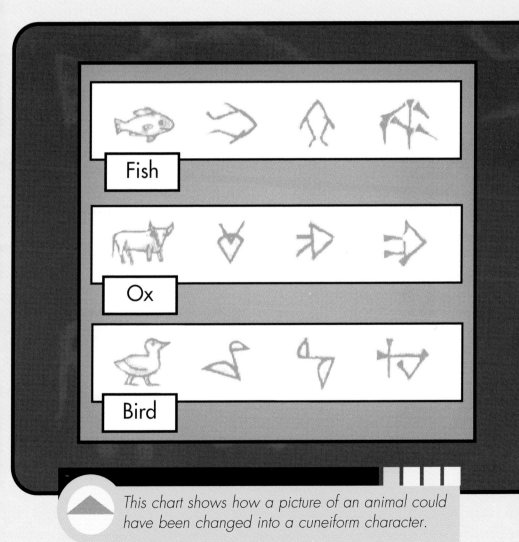

Fish

Ox

Bird

This chart shows how a picture of an animal could have been changed into a cuneiform character.

The clay tablets could be used over and over. However, if a tablet was needed to last a long time, it was baked in a kiln, or oven, to become hard and dry.

This tablet tells how to make a drink that would keep someone healthy.

The tablets were easy to carry and lasted a long time. Thousands of tablets from ancient Mesopotamia have been found.

Cuneiform was also carved into stone, such as on this figure of a goose.

The Akkadians *(ah-KAY-dee-uhnz)* took over Mesopotamia around 2500 B.C. They spoke a different language than the Sumerians, so they had to change Sumerian writing to stand for words in their language. The Akkadians used the cuneiform characters to represent syllables of words.

CHECK IT OUT

▶ *People started using cuneiform to write dictionaries and stories, and to keep records of important information, such as things their kings did.*

This is a letter written in cuneiform by an Akkadian leader.

THE END OF CUNEIFORM

Cuneiform continued to be used for several thousands of years by the people who lived in Mesopotamia. However, cuneiform was slowly replaced by a new alphabet around A.D. 75. People then began to forget how to read and write cuneiform.

In the late 1700s, a rock with writing on it in cuneiform and two other languages was found on the side of a cliff in western Iran. A British army officer could read one of the languages. He used what he knew to read the cuneiform.

Writing changed the civilizations that lived in Mesopotamia. Laws could be written down for everyone to read. People could pass their histories to others by using written records. We have learned a lot about the people of ancient Mesopotamia from their writing.

This is a stone figure of King Hammurabi, a ruler in ancient Mesopotamia. He wrote a set of laws for people to follow.

The laws of King Hammurabi were carved on this eight-foot block of stone. The stone is now in a museum in Paris, France.

Glossary

bookkeeper (**buk**-kee-puhr) someone who keeps records for a business

carve (**kahrv**) to cut into something with great care

character (**kar**-ihk-tuhr) a mark that stands for something

civilization (sihv-uh-luh-**zay**-shuhn) a way of life that includes cities, written forms of language, and special kinds of work for people

cuneiform (kyoo-**nee**-uh-form) a written language that uses wedge-shaped characters

goods (**gudz**) things, such as cloth or animals, that are sold or traded

stylus (**sty**-luhs) a stick with a tip shaped like a triangle used by Sumerians to write on clay tablets

syllables (**sihl**-uh-buhlz) groups of letters in a word that are said together

tablet (**tab**-liht) a flat piece of clay onto which characters could be cut

tokens (**toh**-kuhnz) small pieces of clay with pictures of goods drawn on them used for record keeping

wedge-shaped (**wehj-shaypd**) when something is thick at one end and narrows to a point at the other end

Resources

Books

Science in Ancient Mesopotamia
by Carol Moss
Franklin Watts (1999)

Mesopotamia
by Tami Deedrick
Raintree Steck-Vaughn (2002)

Web Sites

Due to the changing nature of Internet links, PowerKids
Press has developed an online list of Web sites related
to the subjects of this book. This site is updated regularly.
Please use this link to access the list:

http://www.powerkidslinks.com/waw/anme/

Index

Word Count: 479
Note to Librarians, Teachers, and Parents
If reading is a challenge, Reading Power is a solution! Reading Power
is perfect for readers who want high-interest subject matter at an accessible reading
level. These fact-filled, photo-illustrated books are designed for readers who want
straightforward vocabulary, engaging topics, and a manageable reading experience.
With clear picture/text correspondence, leveled Reading Power books put the reader
in charge. Now readers have the power to get the information they want and the skills
they need in a user-friendly format.